CAN I RECYCLE THIS?

a kid's guide to better recycling

and how to reduce
SINGLE-USE PLASTICS

JENNIE ROMER Illustrated by **Christie Young**

VIKING

VIKING
An imprint of Penguin Random House LLC, New York

First published in the United States of America by Viking, an imprint of Penguin Random House LLC, 2023

Text copyright © 2023 by Jennie Romer
Illustrations copyright © 2023 by Christen Ann Young

Visit us online at penguinrandomhouse.com.

Library of Congress Cataloging-in-Publication Data is available.

Manufactured in China

ISBN 9780593204078

10   9   8   7   6   5   4   3   2   1

TOPL

Design by Lily Qian
Text set in Sassoon Montessori

FOR RAINE

Acknowledgments:

Thank you to everyone who helped with the adult edition, plus a very special thank-you to Martha Kaufeldt for her insights into brain-compatible learning.

Let's talk about recycling. You've probably heard that you're supposed to recycle, but you may not know *why* or *how*.

My friends are always asking me their questions about recycling. In fact, I get *so* many questions, I wrote a book to answer them!

First things first: Why should we recycle at all?

Two reasons. First, because the more we recycle, the less we need to use NATURAL RESOURCES like oil, metals, and trees.

For example, paper is made from trees. In fact, every page in this book was once part of a tree! When we recycle paper, we can use it again. That way, we don't have to cut down as many new trees.

The second reason to recycle is
that garbage is a
BIG PROBLEM.

VERY STINKY HERE.

When you put things in the trash
can, they don't disappear. They
usually get dumped into a big hole
in the ground called a LANDFILL.

FIND OUT MORE: As landfill waste DECOMPOSES, it produces
a strong GREENHOUSE GAS called METHANE. Greenhouse gases
trap heat and make our planet too warm, which causes
CLIMATE CHANGE. Often there are pipes in landfills that collect
methane, but these can leak. Other times, instead of
sitting in a landfill, garbage is burned in a process called
INCINERATION. This produces ashes and smoke, and some of
that smoke has chemicals in it that can pollute the air.

Landfills don't just smell bad—they can be unhealthy for the plants, animals, and people living near them.

When you recycle something, it can get made into something new rather than sitting in a landfill forever.

The average single-family household in the United States generates 768 pounds of recyclable material per year. That's about the same weight as a grand piano!

Recycled paper bags get turned into cereal boxes.

Recycled soda cans get turned into new soda cans.

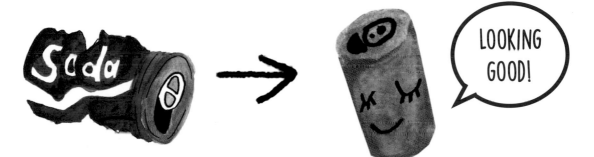

Recycled milk jugs get turned into shampoo bottles.

How does this happen? It takes work from *a lot* of big machines.

First, sanitation workers collect your carefully sorted recyclables in their truck. Then they drive to the local recycling facility and dump everything onto the TIPPING FLOOR.

An excavator or tractor picks up materials from the tipping floor and puts them on a conveyor belt.

Small pieces, like gl[a] shards, bottle caps, and shredded paper fall through. At mar[y] recycling facilities, they are too small t[o] be recycled.

LIBERATOR

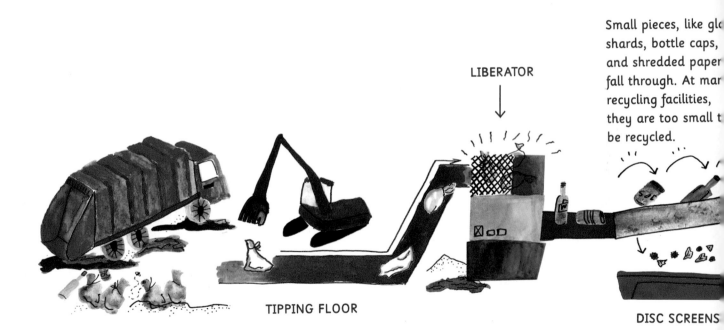

TIPPING FLOOR

DISC SCREENS

In some cities, you can put your recycling in big see-through bags. If you've done that, then the LIBERATOR rips open the bag so each item can be individually sorted.

The materials pass through spinning discs called DISC SCREENS.

DRUM MAGNETS attract certain metals like iron and steel and carry them to their own conveyor belt, where they are sent through a big rotating tunnel called a TROMMEL SCREEN. These machines separate items by size.

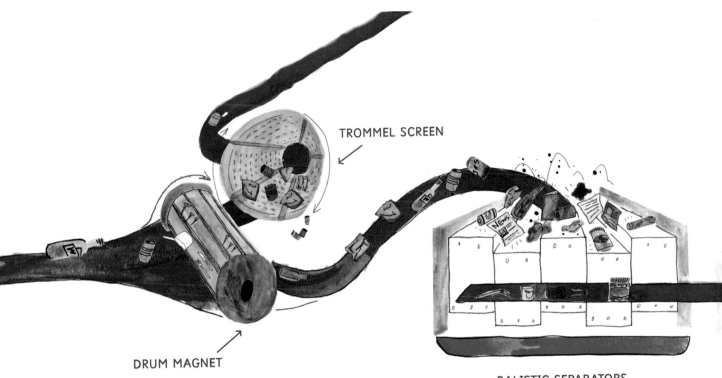

TROMMEL SCREEN

DRUM MAGNET

BALISTIC SEPARATORS

BALLISTIC SEPARATORS jiggle up and down to separate two-dimensional things like paper from three-dimensional things like bottles.

The most important thing that happens at a recycling facility is sorting—lots and lots of sorting!

Things that are made from the same materials go together. Paper goods all go to one place. Glass all goes to another place. In some places, glass is even further sorted by color.

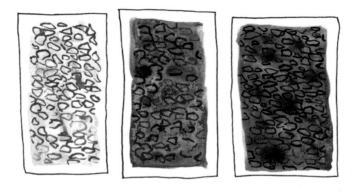

EDDY CURRENT SEPARATOR

The EDDY CURRENT SEPARATOR creates an invisible force that pushes non-magnetic metals, like aluminum, so those get sorted into their own bin.

OPTICAL SORTERS are smart cameras that separate plastic items into different categories. This is because not all plastic is the same—in fact, there are seven different types of plastic! Precise AIR GUNS shoot the most recyclable plastic items off the conveyor belt and into their own bins.

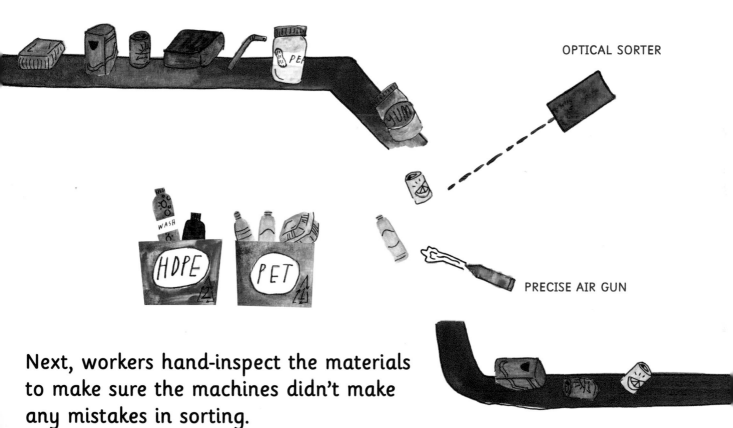

OPTICAL SORTER

PRECISE AIR GUN

HDPE

PET

WASH

Next, workers hand-inspect the materials to make sure the machines didn't make any mistakes in sorting.

Harder-to-recycle stuff goes this way. ⟶

Now that all the recyclables are sorted by material, each material is squished into a big brick called a BALE.

BALE MAKER

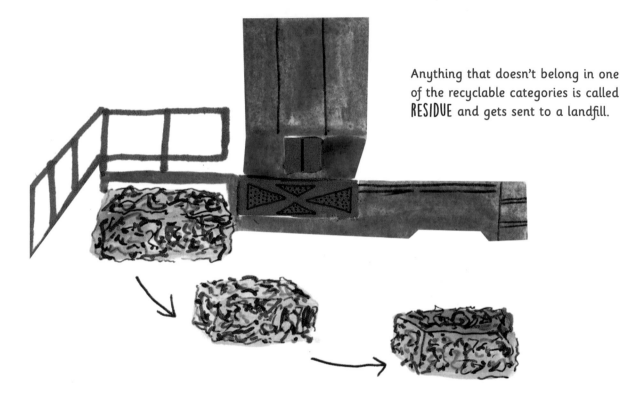

Anything that doesn't belong in one of the recyclable categories is called RESIDUE and gets sent to a landfill.

The recycling facility tries to sell these bales to businesses who will use them to make new products. This means that recycled materials only get made into another item *if* a business wants to buy them.

FIND OUT MORE: Some bales are very valuable and lots of businesses want them— for example, bales of #1 and #2 bottles and jugs. Other bales are made of low-quality materials. Most businesses don't want to buy those. This means that even after all that sorting, bales will still wind up in a landfill if no one wants them.

When businesses purchase bales of plastic, they chop the material into little pieces. These pieces are then cleaned, melted, and pushed through an EXTRUDER MACHINE like spaghetti. The strings of plastic get cut into tiny pellets.

WE'RE CALLED NURDLES!

And now, at last, a recycled bottle has a chance to be used to make something new!

However, nurdles sometimes get spilled into the environment and they're very, very hard to clean up.

OOPS!

How can you decide when to put an object in the recycling bin? I have some tips.

Most importantly: Always follow the local rules for what to put in your recycling bin. Your city understands which items their machinery can sort, and they know which materials businesses will want to buy from them.

If your city's rules say not to put something in the recycling bin,
DON'T DO IT!

Not even if you think it *should* be recyclable. That's called
WISHCYCLING, and it doesn't work.

Small items like plastic forks and straws are hard or impossible to capture, because they fall through the screens early in the sorting process. Food pouches are made from multilayer material that almost no company wants to buy.

Paper is usually recyclable.

Except these:

I'M DIRTY!

Food, grease, and bodily fluids make paper non-recyclable.

MY FIBERS ARE TOO SHORT!

Achoo!

Tissues are made of short fibers, which can't be made back into strong paper.

I'M PART PLASTIC!

To-go cartons from restaurants are often sprayed with plastic coating, which makes it extremely challenging for paper recycling facilities to handle them.

Glass is almost always recyclable.

Except these:

Eyeglasses are made from a mixture of materials, not just glass.

Broken glass is too small for most recycling machines to sort.

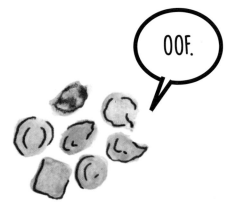

Ceramics often look like glass, but they're actually made of clay, which means they belong in a different category.

Most metals are recyclable.

Except these:

I START FIRES.

Batteries are made from a bunch of different materials. When banged around in a recycling facility, they can cause fires and explosions!

WE GET TANGLED!

Hangers are so thin that they will get tangled up in recycling machines.

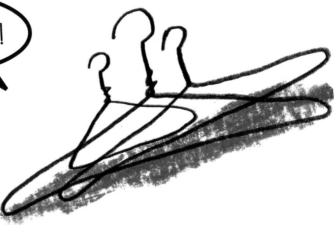

Some plastics are recyclable, but most aren't. There are tons of reasons why a plastic might not be recyclable.

Some plastics are too thin to recycle.

Some things are too small to be sorted by recycling machinery.

Juice pouches are made of both plastic *and* metal, so they don't fit into just one category.

Foam cartons and plastic cups are made from low-quality types of plastic that most manufacturers don't want to buy, so they probably won't be turned into something new.

WE GO IN THE TRASH BIN!

YAY!

The only plastics that are pretty much always recyclable are bottles and jugs made from resins #1 and #2.

When you're unsure whether something can be recycled, check your local rules or ask an adult. If you're still not sure, you can call your city's recycling office and ask!

Which category would you sort these items into? Are they paper, glass, metal, or plastic? Are they recyclable or not?

Because most plastics cannot be recycled, the most helpful thing you can do is try to reduce your plastic usage.

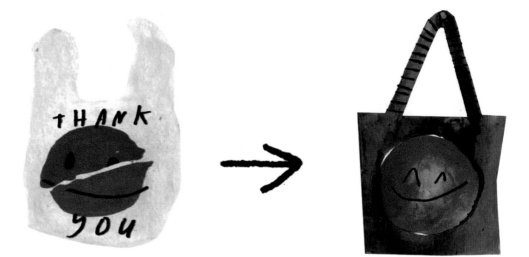

You know you can't recycle a plastic shopping bag, so . . . bring a cloth one!

You know you can't recycle a straw, so . . . drink without one! (Or bring a metal straw from home!)

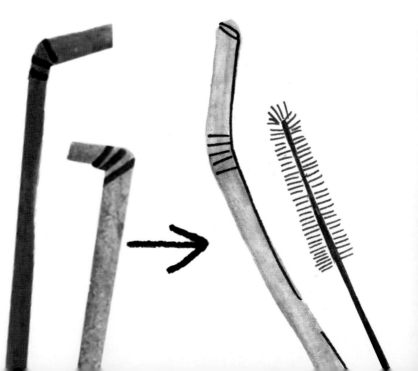

You know plastic baggies are not recyclable, so . . . carry snacks in reusable containers!

You know you can't recycle a ketchup packet, so . . . use a ketchup bottle!

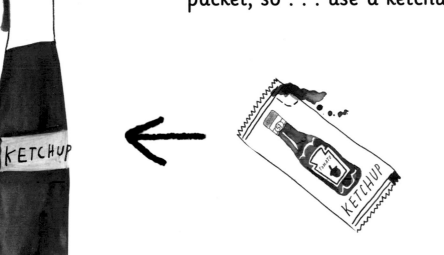

It's okay that you can't do all these things all the time. Try your best, and do what you can!

BRING A THERMOS

HAVE A NICE DAY

PACK YOUR LUNCH BOX

Whenever you can, aim for items that you can use over and over, like a lunch box or a reusable water bottle. You can also REUSE toys or clothing that are still in good condition by donating them or passing them on to someone new. That way, fewer items will go to landfills.

I hope that in the future, we'll be able to reuse more packaging. Imagine if you could refill the same jar with candy every time you went grocery shopping, so you'd never need to waste another candy wrapper!

THAT WOULD BE SWEET!

Some stores already allow you to bring your own reusable containers—ask your store if you can do this!

I get so excited when I think about the big picture and all the solutions that are out there. As a lawyer, I believe that passing laws is one of the best ways to help the environment. For example, some US cities and states already have laws that ban or charge for plastic shopping bags.

In Germany, nearly half of all drinks are sold in reusable bottles that are refilled dozens of times before being recycled. You can write to the people who make laws in your community or state, asking them to support environmentally friendly laws like these.

Hi!
Would you
please
consider
using REAL
forks?

Not
pLAStic

You can also think about big changes that businesses can make. For example, if your favorite restaurant always gives you plastic forks, you could write a letter to them asking to switch to metal forks for dine-in meals.

Imagine a future where all packaging is reusable or refillable, and companies are completely responsible for cleaning up after themselves. Fewer materials will be extracted from the earth, we'll reuse what we have, and we'll make much less new plastic.

Air quality will improve and we'll be able to breathe better air. We'll find that streets and oceans are cleaner, turtles encounter fewer plastic bags and straws, and seabirds gulp down delicious fish rather than floating plastic debris.

This world is possible. And we can build it together.

AUTHOR'S NOTE

Most Saturdays when I was a kid, my mom would bring me to our local recycling center in El Cerrito, California. I loved sitting in the magazine recycling bin, searching for issues of my favorite magazines. That recycling center was a magical place with so many bins for specific items—not just magazines, but also cardboard and other materials that were perfect for art and construction projects. I loved the idea that the things we had used that week would be reused or made into something new.

When I grew up, I wanted to know how recycling worked. What happened after we put our recyclables into those bins? I have learned a lot in the fifteen years that I have been working as an environmental lawyer. I initially wrote and published *Can I Recycle This?* to share some of what I've learned with adults. As soon as I finished it, I adapted it for kids, and that's the book you now hold in your hands. I did so because I believe that no matter what age we are, we can take responsibility for the resources we use and the things we put into the waste stream.

In this book, I talk about some of the items that most commonly wind up in recycling bins, but of course there's not room here for everything. In the adult edition, I go over how to dispose of dozens of other household items. Because recycling technology and policy is so complex, there unfortunately aren't many rules that can easily be applied to every item.

Recycling is not a perfect solution. As you read earlier in this book, lots of things cannot be recycled. And even if they technically can, sometimes they wind up in landfills anyway. Recycling is absolutely worth doing, but it's only one of many tools that we have to fight climate change. Also, remember that reduction and reuse should always come first.

"What happens to our stuff when we're done with it?" is a question that many people don't ask, and even fewer know how to answer. With this book, we've started to explore that issue. Now I hope you'll keep going.

FURTHER RESOURCES

If this book has made you interested in learning more about recycling, here are some ways you can do that:

 Go on a tour of your local recycling facility. If you can't make it in person, there are a lot of great recycling tours on YouTube, including Sims Municipal Recycling in New York City (which I used as my model for the recycling facility described in this book).

 Watch documentary films like THE STORY OF PLASTIC (2019).

 Join the BREAK FREE FROM PLASTIC (breakfreefromplastic.org) movement. Their website provides tons of resources for how you can petition for better environmental policy, hold high-polluting companies responsible, improve recycling practices at your school, and share what you've learned with your family and friends.

 Attend or organize a beach cleanup to help prevent plastic litter from getting into our oceans and harming sea creatures. THE SURFRIDER FOUNDATION (surfrider.org) can show you how to do this.

 Read other books about plastic pollution and how people are fighting against it, such as OLD ENOUGH TO SAVE THE PLANET by Loll Kirby (ABRAMS, 2021); KIDS FIGHT PLASTIC by Martin Dorey (Candlewick, 2020); THE PLASTIC PROBLEM by Aubre Andrus (Lonely Planet, 2020); CLIMATE EMERGENCY ATLAS by Dan Hooke (DK, 2020); WHAT A WASTE by Jess French (DK, 2019); and WHAT IS CLIMATE CHANGE? by Gail Herman (Penguin Workshop, 2018).

GLOSSARY

AIR GUNS: Blasts of compressed air that send particular targeted items off a conveyor belt.

BALE: A big brick of compressed recycled material that's produced by a recycling facility. For example, you could have a bale of milk jugs or a bale of aluminum cans.

BALLISTIC SEPARATORS: A series of shifting "stairsteps" that separate flat objects like paper from three-dimensional items like bottles and containers.

CLIMATE CHANGE: A long-term shift in global weather patterns and temperatures that changes ecosystems and contributes to extreme weather conditions.

DECOMPOSE: To have an item break down and turn into dirt. Natural things like food decompose quickly, sometimes taking only a few days, while man-made things like glass can take millions of years to decompose. Plastic never fully decomposes.

DISC SCREENS: Rotating discs that separate out items too small to be properly sorted at a recycling facility, like plastic bottle caps and glass shards.

DRUM MAGNET: A rotating machine that uses magnetic force to separate out certain metals, like iron and steel.

EDDY CURRENT SEPARATOR: A magnetic force that separates out non-ferrous or non-magnetic metals from the rest of the recyclables.

EXTRUDER MACHINE: Like a large pasta maker, this machine presses melted-down plastic through holes to create long strings of plastic. These strands are then cut into little pellets used for making new products.

GREENHOUSE GASES: Invisible substances in the earth's atmosphere that trap heat and cause the overall temperature on the planet to rise.

INCINERATION: Burning waste in specialized facilities.

LANDFILL: A big pit of waste. Landfills are sealed, oxygen-free environments that are not designed to break down trash—they pretty much just store it in a tomb. But some material decomposes very slowly and releases methane.

LIBERATOR: A machine that tears open bags holding recyclables so they can be sorted.

METHANE: A very strong greenhouse gas produced primarily by landfills.

NATURAL RESOURCES: Materials that exist on earth without humans doing anything to make them. Some examples are water, trees, rocks, stones, etc.

OPTICAL SORTERS: Cameras that use light to automatically distinguish between types of recyclables and then separate the items out by material.

RESIDUE: Any material sent to the recycling facility that was not able to be recycled. (It winds up getting sent to a landfill or incinerated.)

RESIN: A blend of material that creates plastic. Different types of plastic are made from different resins.

REUSE: To find a new use for an old item.

TIPPING FLOOR: Where all recyclables are dumped before they are sorted and processed.

TROMMEL SCREEN: Like an enormous laundry dryer, this machine rotates to separate out small and large metal pieces.

WISHCYCLING: Placing non-recyclable items into a recycling bin because you hope they'll wind up getting recycled anyway. (Unfortunately, this doesn't work!)